T0198688

The Valley of Achor

Omolola Agboola

Illustrated by Windel Eborlas

WestBow Press books may be ordered through booksellers or by contacting:

WestBow Press
A Division of Thomas Nelson & Zondervan
1663 Liberty Drive
Bloomington, IN 47403
www.westbowpress.com
844-714-3454

Illustrated by Windel Eborlas

ISBN: 978-1-6642-6781-7 (sc)
ISBN: 978-1-6642-7217-0 (hc)
ISBN: 978-1-6642-6780-0 (e)

Library of Congress Control Number: 2022909909

Print information available on the last page.

WestBow Press rev. date: 07/22/2022

WESTBOW
PRESS®
A DIVISION OF THOMAS NELSON
& ZONDERVAN

The Valley of Achor

There is a country called Israel, and the people of that country are known as Israelites. A long time ago, they gave an interesting name to a valley because of something that happened there. They called it the Valley of Achor.

That name means "trouble."
Why was it given such a name?

Let's find out.

4

God usually helped the Israelites win whenever they had to fight against other people—for example, when they fought against the big city of Jericho.

6

They had been warned not to take anything from the city so that they would not bring trouble on themselves and all the Israelites. They were supposed to take all the silver, gold, brass, and iron to the storehouse of the Lord.

Now, there was a man called Achan who took a Babylonian garment and some silver and gold when no one was looking. He hid them all in the sand under his tent.

Of course, God was not happy about it. After that, the Israelites went to fight a tiny city called Ai, and God did not help them to win. They lost the fight badly.

Joshua was the leader of the Israelites at that time, and his helpers were called elders. He could not believe what had happened. He and the elders poured dust on their heads and prayed to God. God told Joshua that Israel had sinned. They had stolen some things from Jericho and put them with their own stuff. They needed to destroy the stolen things if they wanted God to be with them again. That meant they could not win any other battle until the stolen items were destroyed.

14

Joshua looked for the person who did such a very, very bad thing. It was Achan, and all the Israelites were angry with him.

They took Achan, all the things he had stolen, and every other thing he had—even his family—to a valley. Then they threw stones at them, burned them with fire, and put a huge pile of stones over them. Achan had brought trouble on all the Israelites. That is why it is called the Valley of Achor.

18

Finally, God was no longer angry with them.

Never take what you have been told not to take so that you don't get yourself and everyone else in trouble.